Athanasia Koutsis

Athanasia is a psychologist who has spent the last decade working along side children who have autism and their families. She has had extensive experience helping siblings through the ups and downs that come with living with autism. Athanasia can also be found discussing the daily round and round with Spot the goldfish.

Gerda De Clercq

Gerda has been teaching for thirty years, the last twelve in the field of autism. She has worked with staff to develop curriculum and strategies to address the specific needs of these children and their families. Gerda lives with a number of lively pets, including Jake "Jump through the hoop" Poodle, who is very obedient, and Marty, the two-legged bike rider (who isn't).

Richard Galbraith

Richard has been illustrating for over twenty years, and is particularly well known for his family of whimsical Australian animal characters. (If you look carefully, you'll find 2 koalas and a platypus in this book.) Richard can often be found exploring Olinda Creek with Suzy - a brown dog with a red collar.

MEET THE AUTHORS!

The autism survival guide for kids

A book for the brothers and sisters of a child with autism

Athanasia Koutsis
Gerda De Clercq

Illustrated by
Richard Galbraith

Published by Wantirna Heights School
Kingloch Parade
Wantirna Victoria 3152 Australia
tel: 61-3-9720 7492
fax: 61-3-9720 7945

email: wantirna.heights.sch@edumail.vic.gov.au

Printed and bound in China

Written by Athanasia Koutsis & Gerda De Clercq
Illustrated by Richard Galbraith
Book design by Richard Galbraith

ISBN 0 646 45931 7

What About Me?

Athanasia Koutsis
Gerda De Clercq

Illustrated by
Richard Galbraith

If you have a brother or sister who has autism, this book's for you!

This Survival Guide will...

- Help you know a bit more about autism.
- Help you understand **why** your brother or sister is doing the things they do.
- Share some experiences of other kids who have a brother or sister with autism.

I'LL GIVE YOU HEAPS OF SURVIVAL TIPS ABOUT WHAT YOU CAN DO WHEN YOU'RE FEELING...
PLAN
SURVIVAL TIPS

...ANGRY, UPSET, ANNOYED...

...WHEN YOU CAN'T COPE ANY MORE, NOBODY UNDERSTANDS YOU, AND YOUR BROTHER OR SISTER IS DRIVING YOU...
CRAZY!
AAAHH!!

But first, what is autism?

A person with autism may have trouble with everyday things like...

MORNING AT MADELINE'S HOUSE
Hearing and feeling...
WRRR....
WRRR..... WRRR...
A PERSON WHO HAS AUTISM MAY SEE, HEAR OR FEEL THINGS IN DIFFERENT WAYS
TANGLES
NO MORE WRINKLES
WRRR..... WRRR...
THE SOUND OF THE HAIR DRYER IS HURTING MADELINE'S EARS, JUST LIKE CHALK SQUEAKING ON THE BLACKBOARD MAY HURT YOUR EARS

Understanding what's being said...

Joining in...
KIDS WITH AUTISM MAY HAVE TROUBLE JOINING IN WITH OTHER KIDS' FUN AND GAMES
HEY SPIKE, CHECK OUT MY PLANE!
HAPPY BIRTHDAY JACK!

Kids with autism may say or do unusual things

Madeline likes to talk and talk about the same thing all the time...

They may not understand what you're saying, or may not be able to tell you what they think or feel.

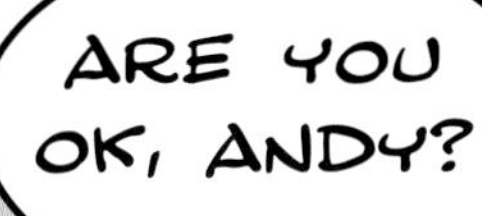

Some kids with autism may not be able to speak at all.

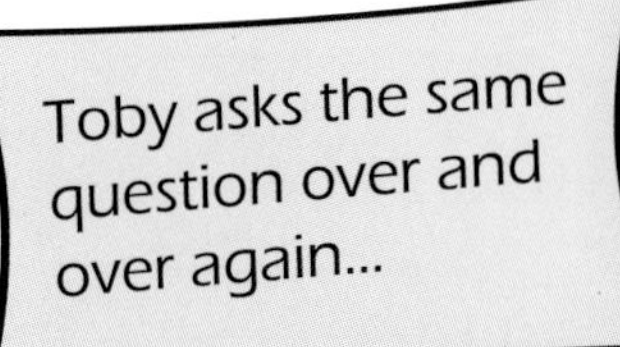

SOME KIDS WITH AUTISM COPY YOU LIKE A PARROT
LIKE A PARROT! SQUAWK! LIKE A PARROT!

HELLO TOBY!
WOULD YOU LIKE A BISCUIT?
HELLO TOBY!

LIKE A BISCUIT?

And Madeline likes making strange noises... in public!
BRRP... BLEEP! BRRP... BLEEP! BRRP... BLEEP!
SUPERMARKET
FLOUR
FLOUR
FLOUR

Behaviour can be tricky...
CANTEEN
Jack doesn't like to wait for his turn. He always wants to be first.
And he can get **mad** when he doesn't get his own way!
And when Jack gets mad, he gets really mad! He starts to...
HIT!
SCREAM!
KICK!
BITE!
But there may be **other** reasons for a major tantrum...
ANDY STOP! TELL ME WHAT'S WRONG!
SRI LANKA BY 46 RUNS!!! AHH! AHH! SRI LANKA BY 46 RUNS!!!
CAN YOU SEE WHY ANDY'S SO UPSET?
whack!
Andy's really upset, but he doesn't know how to tell Dad what's wrong!
HEH! HEH! HEH!

Some children who have autism don't know how to play with other kids

Some kids like to spin things and line them up.

Others like to play the same game **over** and **over** and **over** and **over** again.

Some might not have any friends of their own.

Children who have autism like routine - it helps them feel secure

They like to do the **same** things over and over again, and they like things to **stay the same**.

What other kids say...

I GUESS IT CAN BE DIFFICULT TO EXPLAIN TO SOMEONE ABOUT YOUR BROTHER OR SISTER'S AUTISM
Always want their own way
Unusual noises
Tries to keep things the same
Isn't good at making friends
Sometimes is **very** embarrassing
Makes a big mess in the house
HERE ARE A FEW SUGGESTIONS...
TRY MAKING YOUR OWN LIST OF THINGS THAT DESCRIBE YOUR BROTHER OR SISTER
Things that describe my brother or sister:
A-
U-
T-
I-
S-
M-

What to do when you're being driven... MAD!

REMEMBER! IF YOU'RE BEING HURT YOU NEED TO TELL AN ADULT!
TELL 'EM SPIKE SENT YOU!
Tell an adult...
...if you're being hurt.
bonk!
Put on the earphones and turn up the music.
Tune out
Talk to Mum or Dad about what's going on and how you feel.
Most Important!
SEE YOU AT THE TOP!
24 DIVIDED BY 4 EQUALS 6...
NOT THE RED JUMPER ON MONDAYS...
HAMBURGERS AND FISH AND CHIPS...
28 DIVIDED BY 4 EQUALS 7...
NOT THE RED JUMPER ON MONDAYS
32 DIVIDED BY 4 EQUALS 8...
HAMBURGERS AND FISH AND
NOT THE RED JUMPER ON
36 DIVIDED BY 4 EQUAL
HAMBURGERS AND FISH AND CHIPS...
NOT THE RED JUMPER ON MONDA
40 DIVIDED BY 4 EQUALS 10...
HAMBURGERS AND FISH AND CHIPS...
NOT THE RED JUMPER AND MONDAYS...
THE RED JUMPER AND FISH AND CHIPS...
BURGERS AND FISH AND CHIPS...
DIVIDED BY 4 EQUALS 11...
THE RED JUMPER ON MONDA
DIVIDED BY 4 EQUALS 12...
MBURGERS AND FISH AND CH
52 DIVIDED BY 4 EQUALS 13...
NOT THE RED JUMPER ON
START AGAIN...

The TOTALLY EMBARRASSING Page

"He takes other people's food when we go out for lunch."

"She takes her clothes off in front of friends."

"He makes strange noises."

"She flaps her hands in public when she gets excited."

"We've been asked to leave the restaurant's playground."

"He makes holes in other people's walls - using his head!"

"He takes his swimming shorts off **before** he gets to the changing rooms."

The "TOTALLY EMBARRASSING" List
Write 3 things each that:
- You've done
- Your brother or sister has done
- Your mum or dad has done
HEY, WE ALL DO EMBARRASSING THINGS SOMETIMES! WHY NOT MAKE A 'TOTALLY EMBARRASSING' LIST?
THEN DRAW A PICTURE OF THE MOST EMBARRASSING THING YOUR MUM OR DAD HAS EVER DONE! YUK!
HMM... I COULD WRITE A BOOK ABOUT ALL THE EMBARRASSING THINGS MY MUM AND DAD HAVE DONE!
Mum and Dad
Dancing ***
Telling Jokes **
Sister
Me
YUK RATING GUIDE
Give each item on your list a rating, from 1 to 5 stars.
★ ★ ★ ★ ★
Not bad
Totally embarrassing!

Some things you CAN change and some things you CAN'T change...
YOU CAN'T take the autism away
AUTISM
HANDLE WITH CARE
THIS WAY UP
ROCKET COURIER
YOU CAN learn ways to make things a bit better for yourself
SO LET'S HAVE A LOOK AT SOME IDEAS...
...TO HELP YOU GET ALONG WITH YOUR BROTHER OR SISTER
IDEAS
GAMES
TIPS
PLAN
SURVIVAL TIPS
DIARY

Survival tips for living with autism

Get a good, strong lock on your door. Don't forget to give Mum or Dad a spare key.

Put on some music, either for yourself or your brother or sister.

Ask Mum or Dad to set aside a special time every week just to be with you, to do something you enjoy.

Ask Mum or Dad to have a family meeting to talk about things your family needs to change or fix.
SOMETIMES IT HELPS TO TALK TO SOMEONE ABOUT HOW YOU'RE FEELING
Some kids find it helpful to write their thoughts and feelings in a diary.
This can also help you remember the things that need talking about at a family meeting.
Today my brother broke my best DVD.
Had fun with Jack today TRAMPOLINE
Family Meeting
Wednesday after dinner

Tips for talking to each other

1 Attention
Make sure you catch the other person's attention. Use their name.

2 Speak clearly
It's better than mumbling!

3 Short and simple Keep what you say short and simple. It's much easier to understand.

4 Write or draw

Write down a few words or draw a simple picture to help your brother or sister understand.

And especially important...

Toby's Mum has to drive to school by a different route because of roadworks.

Morning at Madeline's house...

Give your brother or sister a definite time to finish, rather than telling them to stop immediately.

"Five more minutes..."
"Three more turns..."

Doing things together...

"Playing monsters, and every time I play with her I laugh so much I can't breathe!"

"Watching videos."

"Jumping on the trampoline."

"Playing with water."

"Riding bikes."

"Playing in the sandpit."

...and having fun

"Hiding under blankets and playing in tents."

"Building things with cardboard boxes."

"Building cubby houses."

"Playing hide and seek."

"Playing games on the computer."

"Playing with trains and cars."

"Listening to music."

WHAT DO YOU LIKE DOING WITH YOUR BROTHER OR SISTER?

We're all different...

...and we're all special

Sometimes it helps to write down the things that are special about us... just so we don't forget them!

Things that are special about Me

MY LIST	MUM/DAD'S LIST

Things that are special about my Brother or Sister

MY LIST	MUM/DAD'S LIST

SPIKE, DID YOU KNOW DON BRADMAN HAD A BATTING AVERAGE OF 99.94?
COOL!